I Am Not Your Literature

Saniya A. Pearson

Poetry S.A.P.

"For everyone who was erased by the authors of history's retelling, then forced to look its denialism in the eye, it is time to rewrite the pages they took."

— Saniya A. Pearson (Poetry S.A.P.)

Table of Contents

Foreward by Curtis Pearson

In every generation, there are voices that rise above the noise—voices that do more than tell stories; they ignite movements, heal wounds, and hold mirrors to society's soul. Saniya Adonia Pearson is one of those voices. At just sixteen, she had already claimed her place as the 2024 Prince George's County Youth Poet Laureate, but her words carry the weight, wisdom, and fire of generations now and before her.

This collection, *I Am Not Your Literature*, is not simply a book of poems. It is a manifesto of empathy, a testimony of resilience, and a declaration of presence from a young woman who refuses to be boxed, defined, or diminished. Saniya writes not for recognition, but for the underserved, the overlooked, and the unheard. Her work is a lifeline extended to those still finding their own voices, proof that poetry can be both art and activism—freedom with a focus.

As her father, I have witnessed not only the brilliance of her craft, but also the depth of her heart. Saniya is relentless in her work ethic and boundless in her compassion. She pours herself into her community, showing us that true leadership is not about standing above others, but about standing with them. Through her words, she insists on justice, demands visibility, and gifts us with the radical honesty of truth.

What you hold in your hands is more than a book—it is a bridge, a call, and a promise. A bridge between the silenced and the seen. A call to confront the realities we too often ignore. And a promise that the future belongs to those brave enough to speak it into existence.

Saniya is not just a poet, she is a force. And as you turn these pages, you will see why her voice is destined not only to echo, but to transform.

— Curtis Pearson, Dad

The Outsider

I am the outsider looking in

The supporting cast in your movie until I'm caste away

Tucked into a box under the worn shelves of your minds

I find my voice not one to be heard, but rather swaddled in artificial sympathy

A baby being coddled to forget its nightmares

To forget the darkness that shatters it so

The hunger for change lulled with the newest overdue holiday

It's sweet until the bitter aftertaste of tolerance rolls off their tongue

Until we forget our forgotten dreams and the hymns we once sung

I am an outsider

and to many, that means I don't dare to be in

That I am not you

My box too confined and ridged to be yours

Too many continents to be labeled

Too different to sit at your table

That its contents couldn't possibly have any value be
written, the world as misshapen as its lid

And the foolish believe that we aren't connected

That our lines of history don't all needle in
somewhere

But I'm human, doesn't that count for something?

That I can smile, lips crackled with shame

That I can look, stare wide enough to be liked enough
to grasp cold hands

That I can cry, tears spilling books of memories

Pages of pain perishing, engulfed in flames

Concrete housing fire plays

Witch hunts

Crowds lit with bliss

Too blind to see the trouble

and too dense to douse it out

Inked bark curling in pain

Literature lost in the mouths of the dead

Banned ours so much probably wish it were us
instead

I am an outsider

So much so that I can't be allowed in your pool

The only time you let us swim is when you knew we'd
drown

Water plugging ears until we forget how freedom
sounds

How our language sounds

How our culture sounds

Too content to notice the fire surrounding us outside

It's beckoning us closer

Come here child, it said

What are you to live if you cannot breathe?

If you cannot see

suffocating these branches, these leaves

leave us nothing but withering change

I am an outsider

Born by the river

but no water can quench this insatiable thirst

The beast that always needs to be fed

If I touch it, my skin may melt

If I jump into the fire that pools its soul like mine

my skin may burn

It may peel back my eyes

The grass may never be green again

My feet will finally know ground

But would I then know what it's like

to be the insider looking out?

Silent.

Birds sing after a storm

Birds sing after a storm

but if you listen closely, there's a tinted sorrow in their tune

For though the storm has passed, the cloud of pain shifts under another

They look to one another in doubtfulness of their song

and if it is one to be sung for freedom that's not yet freed everyone

A sickening feeling rushed through their hearts, shaking them to the core

as their eyes are traded for another's

Bloodshed

Red dying the water's clear edge

and if you peer down close enough

your reflection becomes one of a caged bird's

Singing helplessly for help they knew wasn't going to come

Slaves to themselves

struggle under those enslaved to power

and the ones who claim they are a part of the solution

become a part of the problem

Longing for the world to change but doing nothing about it

Ignoring the fingers of children ripped from their parents' arms

Ignoring the cries of agony from the eyes that have seen nothing under their film of gray

Ignoring the heads that are forced to bow down

to get on their hands and knees already bruised, and then questioned as to why they don't stand

Ignoring the voices strangled by cold hands gripping their throats with every "can't" and "don't"

until the only thing that confirms they're alive is the thud of their heavy hearts and the sound of their ragged breathing

They ignore all these things shouting to

"Do Something" on blackboards and screens

But ain't nothing changed

and all we're left with is the uncertainty that it will

Time and time again we fight for something that was
thought to be ours from the beginning

Then we raise our weary eyes in confusion when, yet
another voice tells us we're wrong

Black and blue from red, white, and blue lines that
seem to divide us more than unite us

Claiming justice for all

and written in a quill's ink, "All men are created
equal"

Yet those five words still remain false under areas that
may not chain our limbs

but chain our minds

our mouths

But never shall they chain our hearts

No

No

No

Otherwise, we'd be oblivious to the strings of the puppeteer

Knots on our wrists

Refusing to look behind at the sleeves of black suits mimicking our every move

Stating, claiming the storm is over

but is it?

Birds sing after a storm

but rooted inside them they know

I bet you, they know it's merely an illusion

That's why they say *a* storm

for the sun still waits patiently to overtake the clouds

Moving

Moving

Are. we. moving?

Within that question, there's a statement to be made

Ever staying still in the presence of pain

Suffering, clouds of heavy rain

Bang! Bang! Bang! Bang!

Guns fire, hands raised in surrender

A mother cries out through choking tears

as she caresses her baby's head, only 17

Blood smearing their shirt

I ask you, are we moving?

You answer yes...slowly but surely

we are making ripples in the tide

Adding a gust of wind to a tornado of fury, grief, frustration, and most importantly...passion

I see the fire in your eyes burning brighter as you tell me this

A flame of energy igniting inside you

with every outbreak of news on TV

until it becomes a wildfire

One that even the crashing waves of people wanting

us to silence their names into darkness

can *never* put out

Black, brown, gold, honey eyes fluttering shut at the

sound of sirens closing in

A second in time meaning a thousand words as their

last dying breaths escape their lips

Tired of mouthing

I Can't Breathe

Cameras pulled out *if they're lucky*

for others are still left unheard

I ask you again, are we moving?

Feet walking across the streets in search of justice

We yearn for it

Longing to hold it tightly in our clenched fists that
punch the air

for words that have yet been spoken to offer them
rest…peace

And restless we are

Banners held high

Tears flowing

Voices dry from shouting

Crying out together in unison

Wanting there to be equality in every shade

For though we vary in colors and hues all beautifully
made

Red blood courses through *all* our veins

As we stand here today

asking, no, protesting for a change

For if nothing changes, *nothing* changes

I feel a pain that is not mine

I feel a pain that is not mine

A cry that is the farthest thing my eyes would dream
of succumbing to

or that my mouth would wish to form

It is a given that a country where thousands have
sought refuge, refuses to answer when they come
knocking at its door

A mother who has lived there all her life stands on a
land that cannot accept her

Won't accept her because her citizenship encroaches
theirs

For many will soon follow

Her dark skin, the only thing that stands between
them, yet they cannot claim her baby

A child she wishes wouldn't have to be born stateless

No matter how much she pleas for her motherland to
address her as its own, it disowns her

Shuns her

Her diploma

Her aid

Her home

And everything else one might offer if she was of
milk and honey

If her hair was that of a horse's mane

If her accent didn't beg her for air to breathe through
her trills and gasps for a change

If her people did not already blaze in fire

Bodies on the verge of returning to Earth

under the statement that it was not their own

Without so much as a second glance at their pleading
eyes

or a tear when the match was lit

For Haiti

For Congo

For Gaza

For Palestine

I close my eyes and bury my head into the ground
they took you in too soon

I'm sorry

A World That Cannot Be

For every child that is taken from their parents' eyes

Hands reaching for a future that has become lost in the algorithm of our SafeSearch

I cry for you

For every flame that has threatened to burn your home

To spite your siblings and turn them into ashes

To burn your world and excuse it as passion for their own

I am angry with you

For the screams taking your last breath

lost in the horrors tantalizing our screens

For those buried in a sea of unfound hope

I break for you

For what is killing you all

Cannot be called mercy

For what is ripping your pages, your stories whole

Cannot be called protection

Cannot be called intelligence

But calculated monarchs whose authoritarian hides in the name of Sovereignty

The so-called For the People

The ones sending you home back into the fire they call a minor conflict

Cannot be called human

The self-righteous who have adopted a savior complex as they conquered yours and called it thanksgiving

Cannot be called heroes

The men who had thought it best to preserve the
blue-eyed and blonde when they harbor no sky or sea
in theirs

Or the ones wishing to divide their own people upon
a hierarchy to cower and ridicule to be untouchable

Cannot be called leaders

The ones who thought a woman's virtue was to be
easily taken as ripping the cloth of a child's
innocence

Cannot be called virtuous

But cowards who've always seen different

with fear

Vulnerable

What do you make of the vulnerable when they are not ready?

And when they are, what do you do with them?

When the flood of their rivers has drowned the sorrow in yours

You're left screaming to the Earth at the ground you once called home

Distressed, the cool blades of grass start to bristle beneath you

The sunflowers reaching beside you, urging you to wake up

You gasp, breath, a foreign word

Breath, a foreign mother you've missed the lullaby to

Remember melody but forget repetition, notes falter to an uneven rhythm

One you can't measure

And if you can't measure it, does it exist?

And if you can't remember it, will it ever exist?

But how to forget when your motherland's tears brought you here?

When it's her fear that washed out this land

Accepted her visitors' honeysuckle, the sweetness

And it smelled of rotten apple

It reeked of inexperience

of hands falling asleep from covering ears that wouldn't listen

As the "vulnerable" seemed to add too much to her recipe

still, she swallowed all the same

And out flowed rivers of blades sprung of nightmare's bared teeth

Sympathy cradled her absently but couldn't protect her from getting bitten

Couldn't dry or build a dam before it came

Flowing in waves…

it goes and comes in waves, it always does…

The shame

boiling inside every day until blended into weeks

Until the weak struggled to stay beside her any longer

Sympathy still crowded around her but somehow in its comfortability had forgotten to expose her to the ugliness, the betrayal

When they'd soon turn their backs

When the same eyes who sunken hers

wouldn't warn her to breathe through it all

Knowing the heaviness can be hard to bear,

still remained silent when it was her, who was rotting

Her, who reeked of inexperience

Her, who couldn't take anything to numb it when she started feeling dizzy

The bite, infecting her every sense of being

As the "vulnerable" had their fill

and ran away with their thirst

Leaving the children to morn their mother

left sinking under her altruistic ties

What do you make of the "vulnerable" when they are ready?

And what do you do when they leave you to stop the flood?

Retrograde

In a world already spoken for I ask myself:
Is this truly the last of us?
The last time this cycle continues?

My darling, say you will remember me
when all the walls crumble down
and our shards, flaws of imperfection
are all that's left to pick up

I've taken your pieces
The child you once loved
Your outstretched smile
Your sunlit eyes
Your laughter as you'd dance in the rain
and put them in my box of uncertainty
wishful for it to give me some sort of clarity

Now it's just us
A retrograde of sorts
You, the sun and I, an illusion of planets moving
backwards to find you
No one knows how or when
but I know why
I know why we are this way

You were created in a world
of taking with no chance of giving

A world where people sink into the comfort of soil
just to avoid the sun
Its eyes flag yours in spitefulness
Unwilling to receive your shine
your gift

Birthed in a land where they told you being small was
better
So, you contorted yourself to bring them peace
To bring them a sense of relief in their own failure to
dream

See, you are everything everyone wants to be
But no one dares to be
A pipe dream full of fluff
Clouds perhaps inhaled long enough to float away
from their own problems

A sky blank as the canvas of their minds, but a
puzzlement to piece and yet
you are the piece with no clue of fitting anywhere
because
the sun is said never to come too close otherwise
we'd burn
Heat scorching our eyes
Limbs tangled in the web of contentment
And arms sheltered from the blaze of truth

But isn't that what we need?

To burn with the desire to do rather than to get drunk
off dreams?
And yet here we are again
The pressure of others has deceived you to believe no
one cares whether you burn or fall
but I'm still here...

Here locked in this cage of contempt
for being content with the fact that they used you
Abused you
While I
watched from the ground up
as they proceeded to call your type of stand-up
a comedy
instead of a tragedy your legs had to carry the weight
of for so long

You, still the sun and I, the planets that circle you
Some tethered to honesty, others rattled with the guilt
of losing you
Trying in a desperate attempt for you to see your
worth
in hopes you'd grow to open up to me again
and forgive me for my failure to see your pain
I know I've hurt you

The world imprinting its views
onto a sun
My son, child

it wishes to burn it all to dust
Into ashes that'll someday be clouds of charcoal gray
shoved down until
the pitter-patter of rain pours down

I bet they'd miss you then

But that reality check has yet to come
Because they never dared to dream long enough to
make it so
And if nothing happens
the cycle starts once again

And now it's just us…again
A retrograde of sorts
You, the sun and I, an illusion of planets moving
backwards to find you
No one knows how or when
but I know why
I know why we are this way

A lost history

I know

When it comes to this paper and pen, I know you see the difference

Caught up in all the ignorance

Faked like this was religion

The words they bleed like the ink never dried

Like our bodies were never sanctified

Like there's a war going on inside our minds

with no question as to which of us will burn out first

Tired of pumping fists in the air

I wish this could be different

and under different circumstances, you could be different

But it's hard to ignore the blood stains now

Hard to ignore the charcoal grazing my feet

My knees, covered in soot trying to sit in

for who knows how long to stand up

Rather be a tragic comedy than hear hypocrisy

picking and choosing who'll take the next shot at me

Kill this bloodline

Watch heritage become thicker than Project 2025

Watch this worn-skin and balled-up fist soften to crinkled paper

A letter to your flag that we are not "We the People"

And it takes a different type of evil

to light a match and let us burn

Then sit at the table flipping through

water-lily-fied, colorblind stories

Call it glory, an epiphany

Sip American tea and call it a lost history

Peculiar fruit hanging

Horror twists into pomegranate

Seeds of evil cut the thickest of branches

Sprouting minds full of ignorance

And dismantling leaves before they've reached
fruition

Can You See Me?

You can see me

But can you hear me?

Can you feel the history that drags my roots?

The life that tugs at my branches to wave back at you?

To protect you

Watch over you

To fill your lungs to breathe in what I see

The very same air once shared by those that longed to taste the freedom

sitting on your tongue

That rested silently so you can speak

That painfully crawled so you could walk

The trees, us that were cut so you can stand

and walk over the same land I've wandered before

Unsung cries for a voice now yours

ringing in your ear, but sealing itself beneath your lips

Complaining of a dry throat, jumbled words, and a
mouth with a slow leak

So, there you sit with a thirst for change but doing
nothing, as cotton clogs your tongue but, why?

Why do you let it?

Because I still wear chains, I say

I still carry baggage full of fluffed-up hopes

Some dragging an inferiority complex,

but I guess I got that from you, from them

*The cool iron that still chinks, and the loops of metal that still
twist*

That still rusts

Free throws in a game of tug of war

I pray not to lose

I pray not to lose my mind

My mind, they feed it

I eat it, consumed it

Consumed, I eat what they tell me to think

To hear

To listen, listen to the media

To the reading, no, no, not that kind of read

See, in their eyes, it's because they want nothing but joy,

In their eyes it's because they want us to be happy,

to smile

But really in their mind, it's to disregard your roots,

cutting them from their paged grounds

Shoving down queries of what it was like to wear a crown,

to be royalty

Still royalty, and take away the pamphlet that proves it

shows it

Our literacy

Testimonies

Our destiny, destined to be challenged from the beginning

To forget the forgotten

Cover up the pretty garden of secrets left to rot

So, when I finally get a chance to see you

I don't see you

I can't feel you

I don't hear your cries because they're drowned out by lands
romanticized

So, when whispers seep into hungry ears tormented by
ignorancy's arms

it's drowned out by the wind

But little one, you say,

I'm all around you

I live through you

So why do you let them take it?

Why do you let them tell you to swing your legs

Teeter them off the edge of tomorrow

They didn't steal your soul, little one

So why do you sit

and let your voice drip from its cries?

Little one don't you recognize?

You still have the power to rewrite the pages they
took

To narrate your way out of the pretty garden of secrets

To expose the rotting that lies beneath these cotton fields

Little one

I can see you

I can feel you

I hear you

I listened to your prayers every night

I listened to you

Listen to me

All you have to do is close your eyes

I'm still here

So don't be afraid to speak out

To share your truth

Our truth

These roots

To see my branches waving softly and wave back

Peculiar fruit hanging Pt. 2

Peculiar fruit hangs from Florida limbs

now engulfed in flames

I figured it was easy to forget the burning

When the cloth of your clothes was never tattered
with smoke

Rest assure, it was not a just thing that intertwined my
destiny to yours

Tell me, when your family reaches the sea, do you
hear our screams?

Do you smell the smoke under the bitter salt?

Do you taste the souls that ache with no home?

Ache with no bones to tether them to land

They wander here in this sand

Forced to wander, mouths gaping wide

Tell me, do you hear their screams?

Do you see us hanging?

How quickly we were told not to say goodbye

It's why we never say goodbye

But everyone hangs up eventually

Rope beaten

And I'm afraid all we'll ever hear when we close our
eyes is the rattling of bodies who never made it home
to their mother

My lips want to protest for this sound that cannot be
contained

Cannot be sold

Cannot be canned

But it's been preserved for years

My body, a cabinet for the stolen limbs that trailed
the sand long ago

It curls and contorts itself to play the role of forgiver

But what to forgive when a mouth who refuses to
change still profits off remembrance

Off me

the tree still swaying here, its owner buried

and all I hear are screams

Epigenetics/Post Traumatic Slave Syndrome

DNA sequence

begs you to reverse what you've

done to me, to them

Light Switch

My cloak covers up a new bandage each day

Don't know which part of me isn't going to get slaved
away

So, I switch

Like the light was never off

Like somehow my hands held the darkness

I knew ought not to belong

My eyes locked on yours as if my blinking would pull
the trigger

Your gun on my forehead grinning

"I triggered the happy n-"

But I don't see you when the lights turn on

I guess that's part of your ploy

Treating the overlap in my tenacity as reason to hone
yours

Grips on my throat gone

but the choke

The feeling of grasping at straws

At broken branches

At run-down telephone lines

At Harlem Whites Only signs

At runaway starlit skies

At South African apartheid

At scorched synagogues and blue eyes

At language spoon fed 'til we're sterilized

At those forced to watch the party die

How consequential that our cities had to burn like
this

Hands crucified reaching like we were His kin

Now don't know the time limit of the borrowed body
we're in

And you're happy spending it

watching the crowd division

Giving the ammunition

Counting down until I'm tired of reaching

Counting down until the click hits

And only in my time of death do you turn on the light
switch

My History

What do we make of a map with no road?

A heritage with strings of their own accord?

They tug us up, down, sideways

leading to nowhere

abruptly cut from the needle that pins them to home

So, I guess call me Nowhere

A girl with roots no one has ever felt the need to
track down

Claiming "Black" or "African-American" is all I'll
ever need to check that box

The one that tries to shove you into a category

trying to make sense of your "what"

even when you don't know *what* of yourself

And now the box seems suffocating

All the stories you've been told clashing with one
another

Yet you wear your African print, dashiki, and your
Kente cloth

but fear when the time comes someone asks

What country are you from?

Then that dash that separates you from America's
melting pot starts to give way

and now you are just American

Red, blue, and white are the colors that seem to paint
your forehead

Your legs tremble at the thought of standing for a flag
that had once chained your people

The steel that had clamped on their sweaty wrists

The destiny that was forced down their tired throats

and in their wombs

But held no privilege

I grasp these truths with heavy hands

because this is the part no one talks about but still a part of them

The part that many still hate

The part that pins our sisters and brothers against one another

The part that gave colorism its stripes

The paper bag test its strife

And skin color its division

The same

We're all in

The same box

The labels that define us but shouldn't define our worth

Too black, not black enough

Oh, you're one of the *good* ones

Too thick, not thick enough

Hair too wild and lips too plump

Girl, why you preaching anti-whiteness?

Well excuse me and my pro-Blackness

My pro-people-ness

My pro-the culture if that is even a word

No sorries or apologies for being the type of girl

that is sick of being a stereotype

to the ones asking if my hair is real but nit-pick and
comb through what sets me apart from "them"

Us vs Them

More like Us vs Home

And yet here we are, the ceiling closing in again

when my pen closes in on that box again

Maybe this time

I'll make my own

Check "Other"

Not because I have no other options

but because I'm anything and everything in between

The melting pot now becoming stitches of the quilt
we've sewn of legacies

History

Our History

Who am I?

I am poetry

I am the song that dances on your tongue

I am sunflower eyes

I am more than just a box

I AM

I am air

am the soft sound that brings it life

The spaced line between what's genuine and out of spite

I am the whisper of sweetness you hear after lullabies

The tear that crosses your cheek before the last goodbye

Continuous dots after long strands of silences

The needed pause, roots adorned by the quietness

I am foundation so that your feet may stand

But come too close and I'll sink beneath the ground like sand

I am land, I am the sun longing to kiss its Earth

Its shine, too much to bear so we never truly see its worth

I am life, a lost love between breathing's starting and end

The flower and its thorns, beauty preserved by its jagged edge

I am hidden in the corners of darkness blanketing the night sky

I am feeling, I am emotion, the cross of hope glistening in your eyes

I am sunflower petals which carry the honey dew droplets of rain

I am clouds, I am fire, the stillness in the eye of a hurricane

I am reasons, the doors questioning to stay or move on

The chaos in your brain when eyes hold a beat too long

I am song, the music that fills the caged bird's wings

I am freedom, I am peace, the final chord of violin strings

I am the crashing waves of ocean, the calm river's
bend

I am lightning, I am thunder, the curious breeze of
the wind

I am kindness, the taste of sugar before the bitter salt

I am bubbling forgiveness, the silk thread of
memories you've long forgot

You ask me where I am, and the answer before you is
clear

Why darling you don't have to look too far, for I am
already here

Another Perspective

My teacher once said "We were all born with
responsibility

but failed at accountability"

I wanted to ask what he meant, but never got a
chance to

Seems like every common thread connects my
ancestors to you

And I don't want to sound redundant

Already got Black History Month, there's no need to
re-run it

Because you've heard it all right?

The slave ships, the ignorance

Bones reaped for the benefit

Or maybe we liked to break necks for the thrill of it

but I don't know anymore and I'm getting sick of it

Don't know my past but still I bleed from it

You don't even know yours but still you speak on it

Why?

Is it that important to fight for a ghost that never thought of *you*?

Never dreamed of Dr. King swallowing pellets just to walk with you

Never pieced together how Mandela would feel if history repeated

Malcolm X in the back screaming, trying to cancel culture demons

And we feed this

Fresh off the bottle, still we spoon fed

Don't let nobody know what did Scott *Dred*

Don't let nobody know how we robbed kids

Ocean so deep probably don't know where the bottom is

Yet you claim they all live inside you

Sometimes I wonder what caused your pain

and the guilt that drips in my veins

I crushed skulls, you say

But it still hasn't gotten into your brain

of my existence

Heavy-handed on the resistance

Wanna see me die, but don't like this blood on your hands

Forgot you killed, like I killed, when you killed me too

Still, I bleed, like you bleed, but you need me to

So, you'll have someone to blame when the pain hits you

Until you don't know why you mad…

you just shoot

T-R-A-U-M-A

Dysfunction is…

fighting trauma with trauma while the media watches

Reporting live as we grumble about why we're stuck
on the same level

See, we weren't taught to fly

Concrete filling our paths with its cracks, the promise
for better, a crumpled-up letter

Never knew there could be better, so we settled

The rebels of the world have been restless ever since
they got their medals

Funny, the recognition they've been itching for now
in the palm of their hands

What they gonna do with it?

Say thank you to the people who sent them on slave
ships?

They want them to shake hands but

how to be one with something that hated your very existence?

Never did you see the butterfly once wish it was a caterpillar

Never did you see it wishing to trade life in the sky to the life below

So, we sow our hatred into our clothes, our bodies, our dialect

The glass facades that crack

every time another chooses to ignore the true meaning of freedom

Of what it's like without shackles,

strings

Instead, we pulled them tighter every time someone challenges our thinking

See, we weren't taught to fly

Or that we could

They fed our bellies with these lies

Not realizing we are the light of the world

Not moths easily drawn

The puppeteer grinning as he plays with our hearts

Skin becoming weapon, weapon becoming chains

Who knew colors could do us this way?

Might as well be purple

At least that would give us

the tranquility to see

that we hate each other because we hate ourselves,
insecurity

The fact that we are the outsiders looking in

So, we push each other farther away to the edge of
obscurity

Screaming as we drift, on who was dealt the worst
hand

But we were all given struggle

Just because mine is different doesn't mean I never
had to stand

Never had to wonder my worth

in a world that convinces us we couldn't fly

See, we weren't taught to fly

But to grovel

Because the elephant shackled still remembers the rope

though it's bound to it no more

So, rather than clip our wings entirely

we're brainwashed to believe we have none

Hid this from us in books

Figured no one would have the courage to look,

to flip through the pages

of how back then we'd trade our bodies for wings

Desperate now we turn to inhaling clouds of wide eye dream

hoping we'd rise high enough to be with the butterflies

The beauty that blinds people to screech cars into red lights

That cultivates the obsessed to steal joy in plain sight

Those that strategically attack, distract like a predator's death bite

Or the ones that would rather exploit you for profit,
and watch you risk it all for their spite

The same potential churning inside you and I

overcome by their bitter tide

But what they don't know is like dust, we'll rise

and their broken record for better will be swallowed
beneath our grounded feet

For we are the Earth

This dirt that scuffs their shoes

Watch the media fade, getting smaller as we soar

The puppeteer's grin wiped clean

"We never taught you to fly," he'd bellow

And I'd say you're right

We had to teach ourselves

Epigenetics/Post Traumatic Slave Syndrome Pt. 2

Therapy Session

Why does my blood flow through yours?

Why do you blame me?

I never asked for your family tree

And no, I am not stifling your fruition

For I am teaching the brown how to read

under pretenses of it being "their history"

Tradition says I was controlling

that I clipped your wings

But that was years ago

and yet you still blame me

A response to your idios~~yn~~crasy

It seems we've mistaken roles

I, the rebel, and you who'd always do what you were told

I never asked to be forgotten

To twist my limbs to conform this body I'm in from breaking

Shattering into a thousand pieces from every gunshot

Bloodshot

Bodies lay dead rot

No flowers follow them home

I hide beneath all of them, so I don't become the next shot

Pictures of my home scattered on your feed

But I know you'll just keep swiping on your screen

I know how vast this diaspora of destruction is, but to you?

I'm a red drop in the pill you don't want to swallow

The river of bloodshed you don't want to follow

Because if you do, you may find your insides to be red

The hashtags on your #metoo page might become a little too real

Too busy drinking coffee under false pretenses

Oh, hush now, got too quiet now, you feeling restless?

TV already tuned out, part of the deflection

But can't turn it off now to see your own reflection

Because if you do, you may find your insides to be black

Not from the smoke in your lungs

but from the apathy that coats your body like charcoal

Yet never lights it on fire so you feel numb

While I begin to lose the red in my blood

And you begin to lose the humanity in yours,

the love we had for each other when we were born to be something

Now you light a match in the wind just to feel like something

Don't matter how many you'll burn, you just want to feel something

You mindlessly scroll, and it shows you don't sink in nothing

Now as my world burns, all you feel is nothing

Too busy drunk on dreams and it seems

you won't turn into nothing

You say "it's not my problem" so all you do is nothing

And until you face that fact, all your apologies will ever mean is nothing

The Day After Election

I numb the ache before it materializes
Slather it in healing ointment
Anything to brace myself for the pain

All this pain is mine
but all this suffering cannot be

I hear screaming
but my mouth doesn't move

I hear sobs
creaks of floorboard stifled by hushed tones

What is to become of us?

What is to become of *them?*

Who fought for us
Marched for us

Died trying to live for us
long enough to see change

But change is a fickle thing
It is a regret with no end
A question with no reply

I cannot answer their screams
I cannot fake smiles
I cannot do what my parents have tried to do for
years
and tell them that it will be okay.

I feel the ache, a phantom prick underneath my skin
It is a trick, you say.

We are not of this world after all.
Is that why I feel it's against me?

John 15:18

Woman cries

Woman cries

"Baby, where's my baby?"

Over 200 people

"Where's my child?"

Over 200 people are burned

"Where's my baby?"

Over 200 people are burned pages

"Where's my child?"

His brown eyes

His rosy cheeks

His gum-filled smile

He won't wail

He won't cry out to me no more

His eyes stare at me

and he doesn't care for bedtime stories

Says the soot hurts his eyes

Only then he cries for the fire

where 200 people burned

When I try to soothe him

When I rush to take the scorched book from his hands

His fingers grip tighter

The cover, a faded green

These are my people, he says, his knuckles white

And I can't close the book

He, too, was traumatized

watching countless get shot in front of his eyes

And we can't unshake it

Can't erase it

Can't bury it for we may stumble on their slumped
bodies while fumbling in the dirt

Truth hidden under their sunken souls, staring me
straight in the eyes

like his still bore into mine

Where's my baby?

The poplar branches hesitate to reply

The Greenwood Massacre

The Overdose of Dreams

November 6, The day after the 2024 U.S. election

Air is fleeting

I choke on ignorance and fascist beliefs

They bleed into my lungs

Puncture them

It's hard to breathe

But slashing hope is harder with open eyes

So, you screw them shut and take my dreams

Turmoil barricading itself, as a storm flusters around
me

Why has my baby died?

Were the sleeping pills not enough?

The tears pricking my skin seem to agree

not wanting to cradle my last bit of light

I've forgotten how to breathe

Oxygen never knew this stranger

so, it turns away from me

A child backed against the corner

Hands tied cut loose

Still, I sip the glass of uncertainty

and as the marks of a noose trickle down my throat

I take in the redness

It reeks of inexperience

Of hands holding onto ears that wouldn't listen

Of your lips mouthing words that were never written

Of desires to stand up but coaxed to sit in

Of a crime falling for Juxtaposition

Red drips off the hands I told not to succumb to
reality

For reality is often the most disappointing

So, I drink until my eyes grow tired

Until my lungs no longer need to struggle to hold air

To hold hopes rooted in fear

Drowned in the surplus of could-have-beens

I feel you watching silently

Discreetly removing every book from this void room

For knowledge cannot foster in the unlit

And I let you, my back sliding towards the floor

Arms lifelessly hanging by my sides

My sun, where is the sun?

Inhaling but, no longer breathing

The Things We Could Do

This world has hate,
injustice, and pain
And many people out there
are still looking for a change

This land you call "perfect"
is the same land with faults
And here I am writing
still thinking unchanged thoughts

"Oh, the things we could accomplish
if it was hate, we forgot"

Persistent toward our own freedoms
always fighting for the lost
The tired people that protest
are still thinking the same thoughts

"Oh, the things we could accomplish
if it was hate, we forgot"

The things we could see
The things we could achieve
The joy we could feel
The happiness we could breathe
The thought of being free
and the people we could be
All these things and more
that we wish we could be reality

And so, dear world, where is that change
that would remedy violence, injustice, and pain?

To escape the mindless cycle
and release our dreams since caught

"Oh, the things we could accomplish
if it was hate, we forgot"

To the girls of today

To the girls of today,

Our strength lies in our actions not just our words

In the so many ways we've discovered a little light

and made it our sun

Her story becoming ours

Amidst the narrative that had always felt pressurizing
but polarizing

we've turned into diamonds

So that when we pass on our shine, it's flawless

To the girls of today,

When will we realize the power

we so often seek is in ourselves?

The capability of a plant is never measured by its seed

but its care to grow

To know

Shattering the glass ceiling of expectations

The shards we'll use to cut off

the negative ties that confine our strength

and our will

We keep going

To the girls of today,

Understand not every closed door is a loss

And when another has their time in the sun

it's a means of celebration

not of disappointment

Remember we're flowers

no shade, we bloom

To the women of tomorrow,

Be leaders for others to follow

Unapologetically aggressively forging your own path

For what is history if it's not shared

and if it never transcends its present successors

To the women of tomorrow,

Always remember the little girl that's watching you

Nurture her spirit

to keep that fire in her eyes

So, when she writes

it'll be a letter of self-acceptance

When she writes

it'll become a note in a symphony of words

When she writes

her words will move mountains

And when she writes

others will feel the will to do the same

This is for the overturned Roe v. Wade

The fight for equal pay

Our rights were just a pass by

"All in good time"

That's what they said the last time

This is the last time I say

"If we deny this today, then how can we expect there to be a tomorrow?"

Our walk provoking change

Our shout provoking change

Our stance provoking change

Our "see about it, be about it, whatchu gonna do about it" provoking change

So, what is history if ours is not?

What is her story if it never gets taught?

In a world where everything seems to be trailing backward

It's these pages that push us to move forward

To be an anchor for one another in the chaos

When the unending sea of voices attempts to drown us out,

We let it become a wave to push us forward so

To the girls of tomorrow,

Teach them that they have

IMMEASURABLE POWER

So, when she writes

let it be a lesson for *another* to have self-acceptance

When she writes

let it become a note in a bigger song

When she writes

others will feel the will to do the same

And when she writes

her whisper will become a cry for change

COMFORTABLE

To make the world comfortable with the
uncomfortable, is to fill it with more Baldwins and
Luthers

The Malcolm Xs who refuse their words to be twisted
by the press

Wanting us to be the next old press

Conflicted and confused

Deriving from the labels we're assimilated to

We've come too far to still have taboos in our
message

A legacy of Renaissance, Resistance, and Rejection

The issues some still refuse to believe

The double standard, rooted self-hatred, and
insecurity

How grief mingled with brown skin
produced tough love and toughened up

How ironic it is when radicals are too radical,
but fine when the controllers aim at us

Taking out whoever don't liberate how they dictate

Using "By Any Means Necessary"

as a reason they don't see these chains

It's a Mandela Effect

Because every one of my heroes is either a wanted
poster or #say their name
But the ones still breathing are the ones forgetting
from who they came

It's a Mandela Effect

When a hint of light is snuffed out

And the ones still shining are taught to dim down

Afraid

Afraid because before we were ratified, we were
ramified

Now you got brown children, our own light thinking
about suicide

And an unforgiving red pooling these streets

because we've become too comfortable

Roses being cut from concrete

because we've become too comfortable

And some ain't ever seeing flower beds

because we've become too comfortable

Another's roots ripped without remorse

because we've become too comfortable

Confusing this silence for peace

But how many were killed for it and died vowing to
break its hypocrisy?

And when our fingers begin to trace our ancestry,

lumps us all together like clay, all I can do is smile

Watch their comfortable fingers get restless when it's us asking

"Give me liberty or give me death"

because our ancestors figured drowning in the ocean's waves was better than this mess

But Wheatley, just know your memory is not lost

How can I forget your strive through words

when it's given breath to all of ours

And if we don't continue to put paper to pen

knowledge will only be as powerful as we've been given

And that is a world I don't want to live in

A world where we touch on problems but give zero solutions

Wondering if our leaders looked like yours would they still be moving

It's a Mandela Effect

When we forget those who died for the same message

Put them against each other

The Price of the Ticket to being accepted

It's a Mandela Effect

When you know how many are killed for chaos and died trying to ensure it

Died trying to get this world uncomfortable but it's useless

When these waters remain stagnant

Waiting...for us to be the next they swallow whole

Because we've become too comfortable

Moving (Extended)

Moving

Are. we. moving?

Within that question, there's a statement to be made

Ever staying still in the presence of pain

Suffering, clouds of heavy rain

Bang! Bang! Bang! Bang!

Guns fire, hands raised in surrender

A mother cries out through choking tears

as she caresses her baby's head, only 17

Blood smearing their shirt

I ask you, are we moving?

You answer yes…slowly but surely

we are making ripples in the tide

Adding a gust of wind to a tornado of fury, grief,
frustration, and most importantly…passion

I see the fire in your eyes burning brighter as you tell

me this

A flame of energy igniting inside you with every
outbreak of news on TV
Until it becomes a wildfire

One that even the crashing waves of people wanting
us to silence their names into darkness can *never* put
out

It's those eyes that remind me of my brother's
full of hope and light
How I admire the way he sees the world
The treasure in it, the prayer kept beneath his smile
for a tomorrow greater than this

Dear Black Boy

How to tell him that in this world they judge
you by the color of your skin

Dear Black Boy

How to tell him that they see, but don't care for his hope
Don't care for his unrequited love for a society that moves slow to change, but quick to drop a hashtag when yet another face,
another life is taken by the sound of sirens closing in

Black Boys deserve to grow old

My father was 4 months into the world when his father was taken out of it
Police claiming the violence was necessary
My nana called it inhumane, beating him "like he was a dog"

Black Men deserve to grow old

My father's father died at 28

Black Men deserve to grow old

My father's 42

82

Black Men deserve to grow old

But on that screen, we watch as their last dying
breaths escape their lips
The artist of truth paints these words into a picture
that apparently only some can see
The heavy cry of

> *I Can't Breathe*
> *Mama, Mama Help Me*

Because truth be told,
Cameras are only pulled out *if they're lucky*
For others are still left unheard

I ask you again, are we moving?

Feet walking across the streets in search of justice
We yearn for it
Longing to hold it tightly in our clenched fists that
punch the air

for words that have yet been spoken to offer them

rest...peace

And restless we are

Banners held high

Tears flowing

Voices dry from shouting

Crying out together in unison

Wanting there to be equality in every shade

For though we vary in colors and hues all beautifully
made

Red blood courses through *all* our veins

As we stand here today

asking, no, protesting for a change

For if nothing changes, *nothing* changes

So let me ask you again

Are. We. Moving?

Your answer is thoughtful, silence

Head raised as your eyes look into mine

They're still filled with fire,

but now I notice they were always stricken with pain

Confirmation that we aren't just moving

we are going to *keep* moving

Can You See Me Still?

You can see me

But can you hear me?

Can you feel the history that drags my roots?

The life that tugs my branches to wave back at you?

To protect you

Watch over you

To fill your lungs to breathe in what I see

The very same air once shared by those that longed to
taste the freedom

sitting on your tongue

That rested silently so you can speak

That painfully crawled so you could walk

The trees, us that were cut so you can stand

and walk over the same land I've wandered before

Unsung cries for a voice now yours

ringing in your ear, but sealing itself beneath your lips

Complaining of a dry throat, jumbled words, and a mouth with a slow leak

So, there you sit with a thirst for change but doing nothing, as cotton clogs your tongue but, why?

Why do you let it?

Because I still wear chains, I say

I still carry baggage full of fluffed-up hopes

Some dragging an inferiority complex,

but I guess I got that from you, from them

The cool iron that still chinks, and the loops of metal that still twist

That still rust

Free throws in a game of tug-of-war

I pray not to lose

I pray not to lose my mind

My mind, they feed it

I eat it, consumed it

Consumed, I eat what they tell me to think

To hear

To listen, listen to the media

To the reading, no, no not that kind of read

See, in our youth, the issue lies beyond tattered shoes

It's a twisted cycle of lies that continues

Truth that's supposed to hear our cries

now forgotten begging to be rescued

Screaming can't you see me?

Hear my voice longing to cling to yours

To speak up

Ears hearing but do not know what it's like

to have your courage bottled up

To be in the back seat of a classroom

Minds prattling faster than your eyes can wander

To not do it for the desire of the spotlight, but want to feel its

rays all the same

To not be criticized or condemned for wanting to make a

change

It's a dream we're tormented with at night

Daylight seeming more and more confused

For how could someone understand the contradiction of our
pleas,

the way we've painted our world with color but still yet to be
seen

How Dr. King's vision has still yet become more than a dream
but a person's character can drive them to do anything
For it's hard to refute how we've endured
despite those desiring us to lose,
refused to give up instead, stand up
You say

Little one

I'm all around you

I live through you

So why do you let them take it?

Why do you let them tell you to swing your legs

Teeter them off the edge of tomorrow

They didn't steal your soul, little one,

So why do you sit

and let your voice drip from its cries?

Little one don't you recognize?

You still have the power to rewrite the pages they took

To narrate your way out of the pretty garden of secrets

To expose the rotting that lies beneath these cotton fields

Little one

I can see you

I can feel you

I hear you

I listened to your prayers every night

I listened to you

Listen to me

All you have to do is close your eyes

I'm still here

So don't be afraid to speak out

To share your truth

Our truth

These roots

To see my branches waving softly and wave back

Gift & Curse

It's hard to spit out words hoping that the emotion
will stick

That its sticky sap will reach out and soften the hard
concrete smiles I've known so well

It's a gift and a curse to have this hunger

that boils up inside and torments my every being

Knowing simply knowing

when the vulnerable are ready

the cup runneth over

the silence is deafening

the curtain falls

and all you are left with is a broken twig of a person

attempting to hold onto what keeps it rooted

But how when my feet have yet to touch ground?

How, when this rope still twists around my neck?

A snake so enticing at first glance, but squeezes every last bit of hope out my lungs

It's a gift and a curse to have this brain

This heart that fails to beat the same chord and stumbles over progression

Its rhythm, a repetition

Breath, a lullaby I have forgotten the words to

Never thought I ever would need to remember

So, I take on the caste

let it shape me as the tide wanes

sapping my energy as a puppet snips the strings

I still dangle my feet holding onto the broken branch because I've always been scared

Not of falling, but what waits below

the unknown

And kindness has been the only teacher I've ever needed to tell me to remain grounded

To keep going for a child whose yet to know all of the intricacies that flows in her veins

My father God, how He's spoiled me

Shielded me from this world and I am scared of
letting go

Will the drawn-on smiles fade?

Will the giving ever know what it's like to receive?

Will the emotion overwhelm me?

It reeks of inexperience, of sticky sap that draws in
more bees

But honey never knew how much it would sting
when I start to water down

When this rope starts to break

When the snake never mind how much it hypnotizes,
seals my fate

When the vulnerable are ready

They are not focused on the drowning

They are focused on the free falling

The adolescent dreams they've yet to grow into but
still drink off from

Hoping to float

To fly

Even if it's just for a minute, a second

Countdown to

10 years old, I would have never thought poetry would take me this far

At 9 years old, I've always been waiting to touch stars, tryna get my piece of the apple pie

8 what I took for granted and when stage time hit 7, I always thought my legs would have stopped shaking by now

At 6 teen I remember how excited I was to have people who loved me

One year older, now I know who truly likes me

5-dollar bills couldn't buy anything but sleeping pills

I don't know whose story I'm telling right now

If it's mine or yours, which one of us is this 4

But 3 people have reminded me how writing evolves though the ink remains

How a 2-story perspective

Can turn you into some 1

The same person you've tried your hardest to run
back to

She sits, waiting patiently for you to remove the
charcoal grazing her feet

Roses & Thorns

The ink, the page it bleeds

It waits, it seeps with seeds of my own doubt

Trying to figure out where to go from here

I fear I've reached the end again.

I am led to believe we make thorns out of roses

Its sides, pricking our mind's eyes

Clouding our sense of what is and what isn't

and who are we to listen?

Seeping into our thoughts,

a stranger turning this house, once home, into its playground

Covering our mouths and ears, convinced we've blocked out the sound

But how to turn it off when it's what's inside that's loud?

Hands over your ears becoming surround sound for your thoughts

It rains down, the cuts starting to bleed inside out

Flowers we've once knew, jumbled into a fray of I'm okays

Longing to embrace the sun

but we pay them no mind

I am led to believe we make thorns out of roses

The forgotten now shaken with the rug pulled from under its feet

Resurfaced from a child's memories, I feel the hope running dry

Perhaps that's why the delicate often plucks at us from the inside

It hunts for water, to give it a peace of mind

but still, we don't pay it *ours*

I am led to believe we make thorns out of roses

And what hurts the most is when we let that stranger overstep it's stay,

a day turning into a month's worth of lost dream and sleepy-eyed stars

Tired of holding up this shadow of gloom

It, too, wonders when these weeds shall go home

But the comfortable has already settled in its familiarity

It bonds with each other's similarities

Inviting it for tea, so it keeps coming back

I am led to believe we make thorns out of roses

But when and if shall they bloom again, will it make us stronger?

Knowing this rough exterior can be our light too

Protection from those wanting to do the same thing
that stranger did

when the door was left unchecked

and had attempted to break these walls inside our
minds

I am led to believe we make thorns out of roses

And in the midst of adversity, they become our
greatest power.

Because in the same breath, we make roses out of
thorns

becoming our sunshine in the withering midnight
hour.

America is a Deadbeat

A duo piece by Saniya Pearson (Poetry S.A.P.) &
Alexandra Ransome (Lemonade Dream)

America is a deadbeat

A father whose father never raised me

Daddy didn't want me to exist

What's free?

Told my brothers to hate me so when things get bad
and I get out of line, they'll hang me

Sent his dogs after me until I was on my knees

Then questioned why I didn't stand for a pledge that
never sung to me

They try and wash out our history

How the tightness of a curl can take back a word

Because of those curls they'll say you don't deserve
the world

Relax the hair and fry the mind

How do I force myself to fit in a body that America
tried to make no longer mine?

They stole our cells, then threw us in them

It seems in Henrietta Lacks you lacked the decency to
give her body credit that was earned rightfully

They stole our cells, then threw us in them

Bloodied our fingers so yours wouldn't hurt, took us
from the motherland

straight from our mothers' hands

You cut off our tongues to teach us your words

What's free?

You never loved me, only what would come with me:
My DNA, my art, and all that benefits you

But you don't credit the owner of the ideas

Instead, you rewrap broken chains and pass them off
as an exchange for this land

Like this land wasn't one our ancestors once lived on

Like this land is one we'd now wanna stand on

What's free?

We pledge allegiance to our flag

To the nation whose founding was built on the unacceptables

To the wallowing bodies spent like they're expendable

To those whose memories don't get taught 'cause they're not *memorable*

America is a deadbeat

This land never raised me

They claim the flag, but not the baby born under it

Too busy raising the flag to raise who's running it

Never taught us *how to read*

But taught us *to hate our own*

Freedom is the world we want to learn

But my daddy never taught me of this world

I read about it in books

About a place where life is a given, not a privilege

A place of children's laughter

Of smiles and glee

Imagination running free

But fitting in America is like walking on landmines

A ticking time bomb 'til your kin's on the front lines

Then they'll say that you can't do it

because you are a girl

They don't know that you are Rosie the Riveter

 I am GIRL

And on my planet

you must speak through silence

We make Neverland

of the land we were promised

Dear Father,

If only you could see the bigger picture

Zoom out a little, maybe we can make a difference

If daddy understood that he shouldn't see fists in the air as riot,

maybe then he wouldn't shun me to silence

If he understood power to the people isn't meant to show hatred to his but to ask for love

maybe instead of gun violence, he'd lean into hugs

maybe then he'd get that

Liberty is a Black woman

She is more than three-fifths

She will not be compromised

She is we

And we

are billing you for the rights

that were never cashed in

For all the injustice and inaction

For the indifference to our inequality

Liberty is a Black woman

And until you learn that she is more than an
attraction

or a trend to a fascist

WHAT IS FREE?

Acknowledgements

God.

First, thank you God for the doors You have led me through. Thank you for reminding me that not every closed one was a loss, but a chance for better. Thank you for the gift You have bestowed upon me. There was a time when I didn't know where I'd fit into the world, but You showed me my place. Your blessings in my life have continued to surprise, shape, and amazed me.

Family.

I am eternally grateful for the family God has given to support me in my journey.

For my father's encouragement to finish this book. For the car rides spent cultivating my larger-than-life dreams. For the phone call conversations ending in "see you later" to pull out of my pocket when needed. For writing the foreword that opened these pages of past dreams, thank you.

For my mother, whose hope has extended to turning those dreams into reality. For the moments she's been there, through the highs and lows of my poetry life. In so many ways, she has helped me nurture my gift and the 72.8% of me. For being my mother and artist manager (mom-mager): a combination of fierce love and sacrifice, I am forever thankful.

For my grandmothers, whose wisdom and walks of life I've carried in these pages onto numerous stages, you will always hold a special place in my heart.

For always showing up for me and giving me grace… my family, I thank you and love you dearly.

Teachers.

To my 4th grade English teacher, Ms. Claud, thank you for introducing me to poetry and always having a listening ear during recess when I recited my latest piece.

Later, I'd find more listening ears at Central High School. The passion of my teachers and administrators ignited my drive, encouraging me to soar.

To Mr. Washington, my high school English teacher, thank you for pushing me to create new poetry (T-R-A-U-M-A) and always challenging me to connect our conversations to broader social issues.

To Mrs. Jackson, my high school aunt, mock trial coach, and Social Studies teacher, thank you for continuing to support me. The dedication and passion that you brought to class has forever impacted my life. You've reminded me constantly to "be the change I want to see."

To Ms. Holloway, my high school art teacher, thank you for always nurturing my creativity. Every class you always show up with a smile and encourage us to take power in our work. This cover art, *the girl who still hopes for better,* could not have been able to take her seat without you.

It is teachers like you who make growing up in the Prince George's County Public School System a memorable experience.

Community.

If asked to define what a poetry family looks like, it would be you all.

Dialect PG Poets, it goes without saying that you are in many ways a second home. Mr. Washington, the director of this program, has opened me up to a world of poetry and poets who continue to shine. I appreciate every opportunity you have given to further my artistry.

To Words Beats and Life, specifically Ms. Ra, thank you for introducing me to the first class dedicated to hearing my truth. Ms. Ra, if you're reading this, know that your 15-minute prompts have increased my thought and confidence tenfold. You tapped into a part of me that needed a space to grow and did so through your virtual open mics. It was one of the first times I shared with like-minded people. Eventually, I'd find another community of poets who were ready to take on the world, the Words Beats & Life DMV (D.C., Maryland, Virginia) Slam Team. To my poetry siblings and mentors, I promise to always "speak life." To always "see about it, be about it," look silence in the eye and tell 'em "whatchu gonna do about it!"

Thank you to every person and organization that has given me an opportunity to use my poetic gifts.

This book wouldn't have been possible without the love you all have given me.

You are my why.

About The Author

Saniya Pearson (Poetry S.A.P.) is a poet in Prince George's County, Maryland. She has previously earned the title of 2024 Youth Poet Laureate of Prince George's County, sharing her poetry across various platforms. In 2024, she was honored at the General Maryland Assembly, receiving a Senate Resolution commemorating her term as youth poet laureate.

She was honored with the Unsung Hero award from Prince George's County Board of Education, and the Achievement Award from the Prince George's County English Department. In 2025, she earned a certificate of United States (U.S.) Congressional Recognition for her commitment to civic and community engagement as well as promoting change through the arts at the 4th & 5th Congressional District's 44th Annual Black History Month Breakfast Celebration.

Notable performances include Marvin Gaye's 50th *What's Going On* Album Anniversary during "What's Going On Now: The Next Generation Speaks" at the Kennedy Center; the ribbon cutting of Bowie State University's Martin Luther King Jr. Center; the March on Washington Film Festival Awards Gala; Prince George's County Public School's Inaugural Legislative Day; and performing on historic sites in Maryland in remembrance of the enslaved.

Photo by National Center for Children and Families

She also has the distinct pleasure of performing alongside the pioneers of socially conscious spoken word, the Last Poets, for the 100th Anniversary of Malcolm X.

Photo by Zora Johnson

Throughout the years, she has traveled across the country to compete with the DMV Slam Team in the Brave New Voices Competition. Saniya is looking forward to continuing her passion in performing socially conscious and uplifting pieces. She strives to use her words to empower, connect, and invoke a call to action. A passion she will continue to pursue as a civil rights attorney. To learn more about her journey, follow her on Instagram, @poetrysap.

Back cover photo by Bowie State University at the ribbon cutting of the Martin Luther King Jr. Center